Workbook

for

Dare to Lead
by Brené Brown

A Companion Workbook for Individuals, Educators, and Leaders to Using Dare to Lead by Brené Brown

Prepared by
Alyssa Allen

Workbook for Dare to Lead by Brené Brown

A Companion Workbook for Individuals, Educators, and Leaders to Using Dare to Lead by Brené Brown

Prepared by
Alyssa Allen

Copyright © February 2020

All rights reserved

This book or parts thereof may not be reproduced in any form, stored in a retrieval system, or transmitted in any form by any means: photocopy, electronic, recording, mechanical or otherwise without the written permission of the author.

Contents

Introduction 1
   What Stands in the Way Becomes the Way 5

Part One 13
   Rumbling with Vulnerability 13
      Section One: The Moment and the Myths 13
      Section Two: The Call to Courage 21
      Section Three: The Armory 32
      Section Four: Shame and Empathy 40
      Section Five: Curiosity & Grounded Confidence
      50

Part Two 53
   Living Into Your Values 53

Part 3 60
   BRAVING Trust 60

Part 4 64
   Learning to Rise 64

Introduction

In *Dare to Lead*, Brené Brown presents a work borne of experience and not just about putting theories together from Web sources. Brené, in this piece, has practically demystified what it takes to become a daring leader—one with a difference. I believe that you're reading or have read the main text of the book before coming for the workbook.

What you have here is a workbook to help drive the theories of *Dare to Lead* into your mind and make them an integral part of you. This workbook is written for both leaders and aspiring leaders. This workbook primarily contains reviews of chapter summaries and exercises that you'll need to attempt as they apply to you or your team/group, organization, school/classroom, district, etc.

To get the best out of this material, you'll have to be honest with your responses. Where follow up is required, you can use a different pen color to fill that area.

Brené has defined a leader as "anyone who takes responsibility for finding the potential in people and processes, and who has the courage to develop that potential." One key thing about breaking through to become the real person that you were created to be is for you to understand or identify the things that are holding you back. Generally, we can refer to these things as our fears, weaknesses, or limitations. We can also refer to them as barriers or obstacles.

Brené Brown recognizes that barriers or obstacles to becoming a daring leader are real and sometimes scary. She also affirms that naming them can be a step to dealing with them and moving forward.

Right now, what can you say are your challenges, barriers, obstacles, fears, weaknesses, or limitations to becoming a daring leader?

_____

_____

_____
_____
_____
_____
_____
_____
_____
_____

For each of the above-mentioned, how do you intend to go about solving them? What resources do you need? What strategies can you employ?

_____
_____
_____
_____
_____
_____
_____
_____
_____

If you say you don't know how to go about solving the challenges you've listed, then these challenges would have to take the place of you becoming a daring leader. However, if you've spelt out some steps or strategies to surmount these barriers then refuse to rest on your oars until you see that the obstacles are out of your way.

What Stands in the Way Becomes the Way

(See pages 7-8 of Dare to Lead)

Brené had discovered ten behaviors and cultural issues that leaders identified during her research being a stumbling block in organizations around the world.

*What can you say (e.g., instances, who was involved, what was done, etc.) about each of these behaviors in your **defined context**? (e.g., yourself, classroom, school, organization, district, etc.)*

- *We avoid tough conversations, including giving honest, productive feedback.*

_____
_____
_____
_____

_____

_____

_____

_____

- *Rather than spending a reasonable amount of time proactively acknowledging and addressing the fears and feelings that show up during change and upheaval, we spend an unreasonable amount of time managing problematic behaviors.*

_____

_____

_____

_____

_____

_____

_____

_____

- *Diminishing trust caused by a lack of connection and empathy.*

_____
_____
_____
_____
_____
_____
_____
_____

- *Not enough people are taking smart risks or creating and sharing bold ideas to meet changing demands and the insatiable need for innovation.*

_____
_____
_____
_____
_____

_____

_____

_____

_____

- *We get stuck and defined by setbacks, disappointments, and failures, so instead of spending resources on clean-up to ensure that stakeholders or internal processes are made whole, we are spending too much time and energy reassuring team members who are questioning their contribution and value.*

_____

_____

_____

_____

_____

_____

_____

_____

- *Too much shame and blame, not enough accountability and learning.*

- *People are opting out of vital conversations about diversity and inclusivity because they fear looking wrong, saying something wrong, or being wrong. Choosing our own comfort over hard conversations is the epitome of privilege, and it corrodes trust and moves us away from meaningful and lasting change.*

o *When something goes wrong, individuals and teams are rushing into ineffective or unsustainable solutions rather than staying with problem identification and solving. When we fix the wrong thing for the wrong reason, the same problems continue to surface. It's costly and demoralizing.*

- *Organizational values are gauzy and assessed in terms of aspirations rather than actual behaviors that can be taught, measured, and evaluated.*

_____
_____
_____
_____
_____
_____
_____

- *Perfectionism and fear are keeping people from learning and growing.*

_____
_____
_____
_____
_____
_____

_____

_____

Discuss similarities and differences that exist among the behaviors?

_____

_____

_____

_____

_____

Which are the most important barriers to courageous leadership in your chosen context?

_____

_____

_____

_____

_____

_____

Part One

Rumbling with Vulnerability

Section One: The Moment and the Myths

Brené defines vulnerability as the emotion that we experience during times of uncertainty, risk, and emotional exposure. Confronting these turbulent times requires courage and not listening to people who don't have any experience of coming face to face with uncertainties, risk or emotional exposure. Listening to them would only keep you at their level. It's time you begin to define whose criticism or feedback you must consider. However, you don't have to shield yourself from all feedbacks and you don't also have to engage with all of them.

Rumble Tool: The Square Method
(See pages 22 of Dare to Lead)

Bravery abhors defining yourself by what everyone feels about you but at the same time being careful so that you don't end up ignoring everyone's opinion of you. Whose opinion or feedback should then matter to you?

Be guided by these rubrics.
- People who loves you.
- It shouldn't be "Yes" people who never dare for once in their life.

Finally, whose opinion or feedback should matter to you? Make a short list of them.

_____
_____
_____
_____
_____
_____
_____
_____

What strike you mind while thinking who should be part of the list?

_____
_____
_____
_____
_____
_____
_____
_____

The Six Myths of Vulnerability
(See pages 23-42 of Dare to Lead)

Considering the six myths of vulnerability, do these exercises.

What has been in your mind about vulnerability before this time?

_____
_____
_____
_____

In your opinion, what does vulnerability feels like—physically, emotionally and otherwise?

What do people in your sphere of contact (school, community, organization, etc. or yourself) say vulnerability is all about?

_____
_____
_____
_____
_____
_____
_____
_____
_____

Ever come across someone facing uncertainty, risk, or emotional exposure so bravely? When and where was that and in what occasion?

_____
_____
_____
_____
_____
_____

From the 6 myths of vulnerability, which do you think you need to "unlearn" immediately? Which do you find difficult to accept that it's just a myth?

Has there been a time you faced uncertainty, risk, or emotional exposure so bravely? When and where (e.g., school, classroom, organization, district, etc.) was that and in what occasion?

What one way will you experiment vulnerability? Don't forget to define your context (e.g., school, classroom, organization, district, etc.)

Going forward, what would vulnerability and courage look like to you in your effort to be a brave leader?

_____
_____
_____
_____
_____
_____
_____
_____
_____
_____
_____

Section Two: The Call to Courage

Clear is kind and unclear is unkind. Courage is kind and being hypocritical is unkind. You must have the courage to speak; you must have the courage to lead. You can't lead without the courage to speak irrespective of how it feels to receive those words. At least, that's far better than allowing people especially those who look up to you for direction to do things wrongly.

You must also encourage others to speak up too even against so that you don't think that your views are always correct when no one has ever dared to tell you what you should know because they are afraid of how you'd feel. Daring leaders must work to raise their kinds.

The call to courage is the call to putting down your defense to face the unknown. It's the call to putting down your armor. Such armor according to Brené isn't physical but building walls of excuses that prevent you from growing; creating a mental prison for yourself which is far worse than a physical confinement.

Brené in *Dare to Lead* paints a picture of how you assemble such armor around yourself—piece by piece *(See pages 51-52 of Dare to Lead)*.

It starts by saying:

> 1. *I'm not enough.*

Yes, you are not enough because you lack the courage to dare. What more do you need? Nothing!

> 2. *If I'm honest with them about what's happening, they will think less of me or use such knowledge against me.*

Is that what you think? Is that enough reason not to dare? Who cares? At the end of the day, it's you for yourself. If you choose not to be courageous for whatever reason, you will never get to the peak of your potentials.

> 3. *No way am I going to be honest about this. No one else does it. Why do I have to put myself out there?*

Whoever is afraid of the shame would never taste the glory. Again, who cares? See yourself different and act different and from there you will get a different result. Stop creating a defense that would never allow you to move forward. Free yourself.

> 4. Yeah. Screw them. I don't see them being honest about what scares them. And they've got plenty of issues.

Growth comes when you face your fears and surmount them, and not in running away from them. The beauty of life is in the fears that we face and conquer. We grow in solving our problems because the problems would always be there. Go out there and dare.

> 5. It's actually their issues and shortcomings that make me act this way. This is their fault, and there are trying to blame me.

Running away from responsibility is a key sign of a weak leader.

> 6. In fact, now that I think about it, I'm actually better than them.

You think? Okay! Keep at that but what if you are not?

What likely situations can force you to armor up at your workplace, community, or school? Can you mention two of such?

_____

_____

What does the process look like?

    a) How does it show in your body language?

    b) How does it show in your thoughts?

    c) How does it show in your words?

d) How does it show in your behaviors?

_____

_____

"If you are afraid to open a door, you can't go inside the house. If you are afraid to apply same principle to everyone then you are biased and hypocrite."

As a leader, you can't go beyond the things that you are afraid of doing. Brené refers to these things as "The cave you fear to enter" *(See pages 52-53 of Dare to Lead).*

Can you list those "caves" as they apply to you? (e.g., having the boldness to say the truth to your CEO when he errs, initiating hard conversations, etc.)

_____
_____
_____
_____
_____
_____
_____
_____

As a leader, what's your call to courage?

_____

_____

_____

_____

Gritty faith and Gritty facts
(See page 57 of Dare to Lead)

Brené is of the opinion that faith shouldn't be substituted for handwork even in the face of your current realities. Let your faith or dreams be guided by the facts on ground else; you may not get there. Brené named this key learning as Gritty faith and Gritty facts. Gritty faith and Gritty fact is of the position that leadership shouldn't be left for hope or faith but using the facts on ground to guide your journey. Hence, courageous leaders must not only rely on gritty faith but facts as well.

How often do you, your team or group walk with Gritty faith and Gritty facts side by side in your decision-making? Mark "X" where applicable.

- Never   [ ]
- Sometimes   [ ]
- Often   [ ]
- Always   [ ]

_____
_____
_____
_____

How does not balancing Gritty faith and Gritty facts draw you back?

_____
_____
_____
_____
_____
_____
_____
_____

Ever fallen into patterns of optimists and realists, dreamers and reality-checkers, etc.? If yes, what / how was it? Describe the roles?

_____
_____
_____
_____
_____
_____
_____
_____
_____

Care and connection
(See pages 70-75 of Dare to Lead)

" Leaders must either invest a reasonable amount of time attending to fears and feelings, or squander an unreasonable amount of time managing ineffective and unproductive behaviors."

What gets in your way or those of other leaders doing this in your organization, school, community, etc. when referencing the quote above?

_____
_____
_____
_____
_____
_____
_____
_____

As a leader, ever tried to dig into the fears and concerns of your colleagues or students? If yes, what fears were they? How did you address them?

_____
_____
_____
_____
_____
_____
_____
_____

Are there cultural barriers preventing you? Can you list them?

_____
_____
_____
_____
_____
_____
_____

What one commitment is everyone making to begin attending to their fears and feelings?

_____

_____

_____

_____

_____

_____

_____

_____

Section Three: The Armory
(See pages 76-114 of Dare to Lead)

Brené Brown in Dare to Lead emphasizes on the need to have an unarmored heart which sees itself as whole and liberated. Such heart, according to Brené not only sees itself as whole but enough, brave and worthy of love and belonging even though the heart may be imperfect and vulnerable and sometimes, afraid. This is in direct contrast with an armored heart that sees itself as not being enough and full of imperfections, and then forming an armor with those excuses and finally finding rest in their midst.

It is important that we take care of our hearts because if we can win the battle there, we can also win on the outside, and when we lose it there, we lose it everywhere else. Accordingly, Brené is of the position that **"Courage is contagious. To scale daring leadership and build courage in teams and organizations, we have to cultivate a culture in which brave work,**

tough conversations, and whole hearts are the expectation, and armor is not necessary or rewarded."

What two most daring behaviors do you or your team displays?

_____
_____
_____
_____
_____
_____
_____
_____
_____

In the same vein, what two most armored relationships do you or your team displays?

_____
_____
_____

Are they cultural norms influencing these behaviors? For example, are they reward for daring vs. armored leadership in your team?

Think of a shared commitment that you or your team can make that'd lead to a more daring leadership culture.

_____

_____
_____
_____
_____
_____
_____
_____

How armored and daring have you or your team has been?

Armored Leadership

Consider the following elements and select (mark "X") the best option that applies to you.

	Elements	Yes	No
1.	Do you try to be perfect and nursing fear of failure?		
2.	Do you work from scarcity and squandering opportunities for joy and recognition?		
3.	Do you use criticism as self-protection?		
4.	Do you numb?		
5.	Do you propagate the false dichotomy of victim or Viking, crush or be crushed?		
6.	Do you see yourself knowing and being right in all things?		
7.	Do you hide behind cynicism; pointing out the sins of others?		
8.	Do you always pushed to be noticed by others?		
9.	Do you lead for compliance and control?		

10.	Do you weaponize fear and uncertainty?		
11.	Do you use power over such that no one has autonomy of choice?		
12.	Do you reward exhaustion as a status symbol and attaching productivity to self-worth?		
13.	Do you tolerate discrimination, echo chambers, and a "fitting in" culture?		
14.	Do you push to take the credit or collect gold stars that should go your team?		
15.	Do you zigzag and try to avoid facing the main issue?		
16.	Do you lead from hurt—having to defend, compare, and always pushing to be right?		

Daring Leadership

Consider the following elements and select (mark "X") the best option that applies to you.

	Elements	Yes	No
1.	Do you model and encourage healthy striving, empathy, and self-compassion?		
2.	Do you practice gratitude and celebrate milestones and victories?		
3.	Do you set boundaries and finding real comfort?		
4.	Do you practice integration— strong back, soft front, wild heart?		
5.	Do you see yourself being a learner alongside others and getting it right?		
6.	Do you model clarity, kindness, and hope?		
7.	Do you make contributions and take risks?		
8.	Do you use power with, power to, and power within to facilitate growth?		
9.	Do you see it like, "Hustling for our value" instead of "Hustling for my value"?		
10.	Do you cultivate commitment and shared purpose?		

11.	Do you acknowledge, name, and normalize collective fear and uncertainty?		
12.	Do you model and support rest, play, and recovery?		
13.	Do you cultivate a culture of belonging, inclusivity, and diverse perspectives?		
14.	Do you give gold stars i.e. celebrate the hard work and effort of students and staff?		
15.	Do you lead from the heart having compassion, empathy and vulnerability?		
16.	Do you talk straight to a person about an issue or you beat around the bush?		

Section Four: Shame and Empathy
(See pages 119-130 of Dare to Lead).

Shame usually seems to be a threat to our ego, but we shouldn't allow it to overshadow us and make us feel unworthy of anything. However, sharing the things that make you feel ashamed can bring some relief instead of keeping them to yourself. Shame shouldn't be something that pushes you back to your shell. You should be able to face it squarely and make something good out of it.

What causes you shame especially as a leader?

_____
_____
_____
_____
_____
_____
_____
_____

How do you respond to shame?

_____
_____
_____
_____
_____
_____
_____
_____

In the past, have you because of shame become afraid of forging ahead and instead withdrawn into yourself?

_____
_____
_____
_____
_____
_____

_____

_____

Would you prefer to protect your ego instead of opening up on something you don't know so that you can learn something new? Mark "X" where applicable.

Yes [ ]   No [ ]

As pointed out by Brené, with understanding and awareness, we are less likely going to need shame shields and responding to shame in a manner that affects our aspirations is a form of armored leadership.

"Empathy is connecting to the emotions that underpin an experience."
(See pages 136-150 of Dare to Lead).

Ever tried to share something that makes you feel ashamed with someone else? If yes, how was the feeling when light was shed on the matter for you?

_____

_____

_____

_____

_____

_____

_____

_____

If you share your problems with others and you don't get satisfying responds, would you like to tell people about new problems you may be facing again? Mark "X" where applicable.

Yes [ ]   No [ ]

Do you think keeping your problems to yourself to protect your ego can have a negative impact on your ability to excel in life?

Yes [ ]   No [ ]

Empathy in Practice

Brené has listed some empathy misses to include;

1. Sympathy vs. Empathy.
2. The Gasp and Awe.
3. The Mighty Fall.
4. The Block and Tackle.
5. The Boots and Shovel.

6. If You Think That's Bad.

From the above empathy misses:

Which do you use and needs to change?
_____
_____
_____
_____
_____
_____
_____

Which from the list of the empathy misses shut you down?
_____
_____
_____
_____
_____
_____
_____

How can you rate your empathic skill?

_____
_____
_____
_____
_____
_____
_____
_____
_____

Shame Shields: How do you try to avoid shame?
(See page 161 of Dare to Lead)

In trying to avoid shame, do you:

Move away?   Yes [ ]   No [ ]
Moving away involves hiding, withdrawing, silencing ourselves and keeping secrets.

Whom would you most likely invoke this shield for?

_____
_____
_____
_____
_____
_____
_____

What situations can prompt you to invoke this shield either at workplace, school, or anywhere?

_____
_____
_____
_____
_____
_____
_____

Move forward? Yes [ ]   No [ ]
Like trying to appease and please.

Whom would you most likely invoke this shield for?
_____
_____
_____
_____
_____
_____
_____
_____

What situations can prompt you to invoke this shield either at workplace, school, or anywhere?
_____
_____
_____
_____
_____
_____
_____

Move against? Yes [ ] No [ ]
This involves becoming aggressive and trying to power over or using shame to fight shame.

Whom would you most likely invoke this shield for?

What situations can prompt you to invoke this shield either at workplace, school, or anywhere?

Any other kind of shield not mentioned here? Name and explain how you use them.

Section Five: Curiosity & Grounded Confidence

(See pages 171-174 of Dare to Lead)

Grounded Confidence = Rumble Skills + Curiosity + Practice

Leading effectively requires that we seek, respect and leverage the views of others and stay curious. Being curious can help unearth a lot of information and ideas.

Find below curiosity tips to a hard conversation with yourself or others.

1. The story I make up . . .
2. I'm curious about . . .
3. Tell me more.
4. That's not my experience (instead of "You're wrong about her, him, them, it, this . . .").
5. I'm wondering . . .
6. Help me understand . . .
7. Walk me through . . .
8. We're both dug in. Tell me about your passion around this.

9. Tell me why this doesn't fit/work for you.

10. I'm working from these assumptions—what about you?

11. What problem are we trying to solve?

From the above,

Which seems organic to the way you lean into hard conversations?

_____
_____
_____
_____
_____

What more curiosity tips can you come up with that can lead you to a hard conversation?

_____
_____
_____
_____
_____
_____

Horizon conflict
(See page 174 of Dare to Lead)

What two or more potential horizon conflicts can you identify from a recent project?

_____
_____
_____
_____
_____
_____
_____

How can you handle horizon conflict if it shows up in your team? Right now, how do you see it showing up?

_____
_____
_____
_____
_____
_____
_____

Part Two

Living Into Your Values

(See pages 185-190 of Dare to Lead)

From the list of values in *Dare to Lead,* which beliefs are most important to you?

1. _____

2. _____

Note that the values you have listed should be able to,
- Define you.
- Tell that these values define who you are at best.
- Does the value(s) reflect what usually helps you to make tough decisions?

Going further:

Restate your value #1:

_____
_____

What behaviors support this value?

___

___

___

What behaviors do not support this value?

___

___

___

At what point in time did you yield completely into this value?

___

___

___

Who within your sphere of contact encourages you to live into this value?

___

___

___

What does their encouragement look like?

___

___

___

How do you appreciate yourself as you live into this value?

_____

_____

_____

Can you identify warning behaviors that suggest you are diverting from this value?

_____

_____

_____

Can you describe that feeling seeing yourself yielding to your values?

_____

_____

_____

How does this value shape how you give and receive feedback from others?

_____

_____

_____

What more support do you need to live into this value?

_____
_____

Restate your value #2:

_____
_____

What behaviors support this value?

_____
_____
_____

What behaviors do not support this value?

_____
_____
_____

At what point in time did you yield completely into this value?

_____
_____
_____

Who within your sphere of contact encourages you to live into this value?

_____
_____
_____

What does their encouragement look like?

_____
_____
_____

How do you appreciate yourself as you live into this value?

_____
_____
_____

Can you identify warning behaviors that suggest you are diverting from this value?

_____
_____
_____

Can you describe that feeling seeing yourself yielding to your values?

_____

_____

_____

How does this value shape how you give and receive feedback from others?

_____

_____

_____

What more support do you need to live into this value?

_____

_____

_____

Engaged Feedback Checklist
(See pages 198-207 of Dare to Lead)

Feedback: How, when and why

How helpful is the engaged feedback checklist to you or your team?

_____
_____
_____
_____
_____

What perfectly fits you or your team from the checklist?

_____
_____
_____
_____
_____

What's working about your feedback sharing and what's not working?

_____
_____
_____
_____
_____

Part 3

BRAVING Trust

(See pages 224-233 of Dare to Lead)

In Dare to Lead, BRAVING is an acronym for boundaries (B), reliability (R), accountability (A), vault (V), integrity (I), non-judgment (N), and generosity (G). In this exercise, we'll look at how you can operationalize trust through brazing.

Part 1: Frequency of delivery.

How frequent do you deliver on this element? Mark X where applicable.

Boundaries
Rarely	[ ]
Sometimes	[ ]
Often	[ ]
Always	[ ]

Reliability
Rarely	[ ]
Sometimes	[ ]
Often	[ ]
Always	[ ]

Accountability
Rarely   [ ]
Sometimes   [ ]
Often   [ ]
Always   [ ]

Vault
Rarely   [ ]
Sometimes   [ ]
Often   [ ]
Always   [ ]

Integrity
Rarely   [ ]
Sometimes   [ ]
Often   [ ]
Always   [ ]

Non-judgment
Rarely   [ ]
Sometimes   [ ]
Often   [ ]
Always   [ ]

Generosity
Rarely   [ ]
Sometimes   [ ]
Often   [ ]
Always   [ ]

Part 2: Linking BRAVING to behaviors

Based on your choices in part 1, write down your behaviors that speaks directly to the elements.

Boundaries
_____
_____

Reliability
_____
_____

Accountability
_____
_____

Vault
_____
_____

Integrity
_____
_____

Non-judgement
_____
_____

Generosity
_____
_____

What behavior are you willing to commit to for each element for you and for your team / organization?

Boundaries

_____

_____

Reliability

_____

_____

Accountability

_____

_____

Vault

_____

_____

Integrity

_____

_____

Non-judgement

_____

_____

Part 4

Learning to Rise

(See pages 249-251 of Dare to Lead)

When emotion seems to take advantage of you, how can you reorganize? A few examples of those times when get hooked by emotion include a) difficulty in coming out of your skin, b) playing events on a loop, etc.

How do you react when grabbed by emotion?
Body: How do you physically feel?
_____
_____

Mind: What do you think?
_____
_____

Behavior: How do you behave as a result of being grabbed by emotion?
_____
_____

Story: What stories do you make up during this time? What are they about?

_____

_____

Reorganizing your offloading strategy
(See pages 251-255 of Dare to Lead)

Strategy 1: Chandeliering

Is this a common strategy you adopt to offload?

Yes [ ]   No [ ]

How does it feel when others adopt this strategy to offload with you?

_____

_____

_____

_____

How does this strategy impact you or your organization's culture?

_____

_____

_____

_____

Strategy 2: Bouncing Hurt

Is this a common strategy you adopt to offload?

Yes [ ]   No [ ]

How does it feel when others adopt this strategy to offload with you?

_____
_____
_____
_____

How does this strategy impact you or your organization's culture?

_____
_____
_____
_____

Strategy 3: Numbing

Is this a common strategy you adopt to offload?

Yes [ ]   No [ ]

How does it feel when others adopt this strategy to offload with you?

_____

_____

_____

_____

How does this strategy impact you or your organization's culture?

_____

_____

_____

_____

Strategy 4: Stockpiling Hurt

Is this a common strategy you adopt to offload?

Yes [ ]   No [ ]

How does it feel when others adopt this strategy to offload with you?

_____

_____

_____

_____

How does this strategy impact you or your organization's culture?

_____
_____
_____

Strategy 5: The Umbridge

Is this a common strategy you adopt to offload?

Yes [ ]   No [ ]

How does it feel when others adopt this strategy to offload with you?

_____
_____
_____

How does this strategy impact you or your organization's culture?

_____
_____
_____

Strategy 6: Hurt and the fear of high-centering

Is this a common strategy you adopt to offload?

Yes [ ]   No [ ]

How does it feel when others adopt this strategy to offload with you?

_____
_____
_____
_____

How does this strategy impact you or your organization's culture?

_____
_____
_____
_____

The Reckoning, The Rumble, and The Revolution.
(See pages 258-268 of Dare to Lead)

Putting together all three processes (the reckoning, rumble and revolution) and measuring the impact on your organization.

What are your falls?
_____
_____
_____
_____

How did you know you were hooked by emotion? Is there something you couldn't stop thinking about?
_____
_____
_____
_____

How did you offload hurt? (You didn't?)
_____
_____
_____
_____

Conspiracies and confabulations

_____
_____
_____
_____

Did your SFD push you to dig into something? What were they?

_____
_____
_____
_____

What more did you need to learn about the story and those that formed it?

_____
_____
_____
_____

Did you need to look at something in yourself? What was it?

_____
_____
_____
_____

What emotions did you need to rumble with? (e.g. forgiveness, anxiety, grief, boundaries, criticism, guilt, trust, vulnerability, shame, etc.)

_____
_____
_____
_____

What's your brave new ending?

_____
_____
_____
_____

What key learnings have you derived?

_____
_____

Has this process changed you as a person and leader?

RECOMMENDATIONS

GRATITUDE JOURNAL
https://amazon.com/dp/1651107564

ACADEMIC PLANNER FOR STUDENTS
https://amazon.com/dp/1792619367

RECURRING SUBSCRIPTION LOG BOOK
https://amazon.com/dp/B08457LMJ6

DAILY PLANNER FOR NOTEBOOK
https://amazon.com/dp/1725520087

INTERNET ADDRESS AND PASSWORD LOG BOOK
https://amazon.com/dp/B083XVJG32

Made in the USA
Monee, IL
25 February 2020